SOCCER
FUNDAMENTALS

SOCCER FUNDAMENTALS

Basic Skills, Drills, and Strategy for Beginning Players

by John Learmouth

Artwork by Bob Hogarth
Photographs by Brian Raven

St. Martin's Press, New York

By the same author
THE YOUNG GYMNAST

ISBN 0-312-11532-6

10   9   8   7   6   5   4   3   2   1

9540

Contents

This book is dedicated to all those American young-sters who are in the process of discovering the joys of soccer—the activity that Pelé describes as "the beautiful game."

Acknowledgments

My grateful thanks are due to my wife Gwen, who, as my coauthor, has done all the research and all the other unglamorous but vital work that kept me supplied with working material. They are also due to Brian Raven for the photographs, to Bob Hogarth for the artwork, and to Joyce Braithwaite for producing the manuscript in record time. My especial thanks go to:

John Dunne
Craig Halstead   of Warley Road Junior School,
Neil Jepson   Halifax
Richard Smith

Simon Bairstow
Paul Dunn   of Holy Trinity (C.E.) Junior School,
Andrew Ingle   Halifax
Philip Orrell

Anthony Lewis
Nicholas Richardson   of St. Mary's (R.C.) Junior School,
Jeremy Starsmore   Halifax

Rainford Bowley   of J.H. Whitleu Secondary School,
                        Halifax
Gary Hughes   of Sowerby Bridge Grammar School,
                        Halifax
who endured the discomforts of several very cold winter
days when we had the photographs taken.

   Thanks also to Mitre Sports Ltd. of Huddersfield,
England, for supplying the Multiplex and Mouldmaster
balls and the soccer shoes for the boys.

J. K. L.
Huddersfield
England

APRIL 1978

SOCCER FUNDAMENTALS

About the Game

"Soccer" is a funny word, and certainly a strange name for a game. The names of other games usually tell you something about the game. For instance, basketball suggests that the game has something to do with a ball and a basket; baseball tells you that the game is concerned with bases and a ball. But "soccer" tells you nothing about the game. The word "soccer" is English schoolboy slang, from the last century. This is how the game came to be known by that name.

In England, a school which is called a public school is, in fact, a private school—usually a boarding school— and parents pay high fees to enable their children to attend such schools. In the middle of the last century, team ball games formed the entire physical education program in the public schools, and during the winter, they all played football. Each school had its own type of football: some played a kind of football where the ball was an oval sort of shape, and was mostly *handled* rather than kicked. Others used a ball which was nearer in shape to being round, and which was *kicked* most of the time, but sometimes handled. Some schools had rules concerning how many players should play in each team, while others allowed a team to field as many players as it could find.

Many of the boys from these schools went on to college, Oxford or Cambridge, and they wanted to continue playing football as a pastime. However, since they all came from different schools, they could not agree on how the game should be played. They all wanted to play according to the rules of their former schools. Eventually, a group of students from schools where football had been a game where the ball was mainly kicked agreed to a set of rules so that they could form teams and play matches. This happened at Cambridge, and, shortly afterward, in 1863, a meeting of followers of the kicking game got together in

London and formed the Football Association, which became the ruling body of the game in England, and the model for other national associations.

An interesting side effect of this was that, at the time the Football Association was formed, those who preferred the handling type of football found themselves outside the Association, and with no fixed set of rules under which they could play. They then got together and formed a "union" of those who wished to play the handling game in a manner similar to the way it was played at Rugby School. Thus was formed The Rugby Football Union, which became the governing body for the handling game as it was, and still is, played in England and other parts of the world.

At that time, a favorite form of slang among public schoolboys and the alumni of these public schools was to shorten a word and then add "er" to the end of it. Using this slang, they called breakfast "brekker," a preparatory school was a "prepper," and so on. And so, quite naturally, Rugby Football became "rugger" and Association Football became known as "Assocc" and then "soccer."

If you think of all the different forms of football that you may know—American Football, Association Football, Gaelic Football, Rugby Football, Australian Rules Football, and so on-you might think it rather strange that they are all called football, when, in fact, Association Football, or soccer, is the only one where the game mainly involves kicking a ball with the foot. All the others concentrate more on running with the ball in the hands and passing it from hand to hand. In many countries, particularly on the continent of Europe, soccer is called football, but that is probably because the countries concerned have not got another form of football game of their own.

The organization which controls soccer throughout the world is the *Fédération Internationale de Football Association*, generally known as FIFA. Any country may have its own rules for soccer, but if a team from one country wishes to play against a team from another country, then both teams must play under FIFA rules. What FIFA has done is exactly the same as what that first Association did in England, in 1863: it has made sure everyone plays under the same rules, throughout the world.

The rules of soccer are simple, and there are not many of them. This is one of the reasons why so many people all over the world play soccer, or watch it, as spectators. Because there are not too many rules, the referee is not continually blowing his whistle to stop play, and so the game flows, and this makes it fun to watch. Of course, there used to be all sorts of rules saying things like, "players must remove their hats before heading the ball"—necessary in the early days because all the players would wear hats of different kinds when playing. Nowadays, however, the rules are easy to understand and remember. When you start playing, all you really need to know is that:

1. When play is going on, no player except the goalkeeper is allowed to touch the ball with his hand or arm;
2. No player may hit, kick, trip, push, or jump at another player;
3. The playing area should be marked like this:

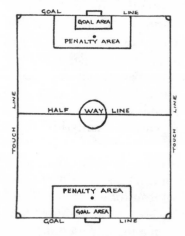

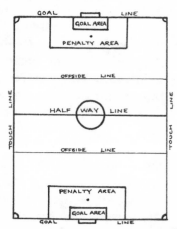

PLAYING PITCH F·I·F·A· REGULATIONS   PLAYING PITCH N·A·S·L· REGULATIONS

The rules of the North American Soccer League require the inclusion of an extra line in each half of the field, thirty-five yards from the goal line. These are "offside lines" and an attacking player can only be offside, under NASL rules, if he is between the offside line and the goal he is attacking when the ball is played. This is different from the FIFA offside rule, which says that a player is offside if he is between the center line and the goal he is attacking when the ball is played.

Also, the NASL rules call for a "shoot out" to decide the result of a game which is tied at the end of the normal period of playing time. FIFA rules do not allow the "shoot out." Thus, the final result of a game under NASL rules cannot be a tie, while under FIFA rules it can. There are eleven players on a full team. I use the term "full team" because there is nothing to prevent playing the game with a smaller number of players on each team. Seven, six, or five on a team are very popular numbers for boys' games.

A full team may adopt any one of several playing formations. The position of the goalkeeper is fixed, because he has to guard the goal, but the other ten players may be positioned either in a 4−2−4 formation, like this:

Goalkeeper

Right Fullback   Right Center Back   Left Center Back   Left Fullback

Right Midfield   Left Midfield

Right Winger   Striker   Striker   Left Winger

or a 4−3−3 formation, like this:

Goalkeeper

Right Fullback   Right Center Back   Left Center Back   Left Fullback

Right Midfield   Center Midfield   Left Midfield

Striker   Striker   Striker

or a 4−4−2 formation, like this:

Goalkeeper

Right Fullback   Right Center Back   Left Center Back   Left Fullback

Right Midfield 1   Right Midfield 2   Left Midfield 1   Left Midfield 2

Striker   Striker

The formation that a team adopts is decided according to the strengths and weaknesses of its players, the strengths and weaknesses of its opponents, and the overall policy for the match—that is, mainly attacking or mainly defensive. There is no magic about any system. No single system can make a poor team good. Any system can be only as good as the players using it. You will see many variations of these systems—and some that are totally different.

Any system that any team uses or invents, however, is built on the various players:

1. A goalkeeper;
2. Players who have special defensive skills. (These are the "backs" and they form the line of defense in front of the goal. Many of them also possess first-class attacking skills, which they use as the situation demands.);
3. Players who have both attacking and defendingskills. (These midfield players must have the stamina to assist in an attack at one minute, and be a hundred yards back the next minute, helping out with the defense. They must also be very skilled in setting up attacking situations, because most attacks start from the midfield.);
4. Players with special attacking skills. (These are the front line of attack, and may be known as "strikers," or sometimes as "wingers" if they operate mainly along the sides of the field. The strikers and wingers are expected to score most of the goals.)

The only true specialist, however, is the goalkeeper. The rules of the game fix his position so that he really cannot do anything other than use his goalkeeping skills, while the other ten players have to consider themselves as interchangeable, no matter what special skills they have. A back who cannot set up, take part in, and sometimes finish off an attack is only half a player. The same is true of a striker who cannot play an effective defensive role when necessary. It is often said in soccer that the team that controls the middle of the playing field wins. This means that the midfield players have got to be able both to win the ball in the tackle and then make good use of it to set up an attack.

It is a great mistake for any young player to tie a label on himself as, say, a striker or a center back. Many of the greatest players started their careers in a different position from the one in which they achieved real success. Aim to become a good soccer player first, and try out for different positions. Never be afraid to try a new one. Pele, Bobby Moore, and Franz Beckenbauer would all have been great players in *any* position.

PLAYING EQUIPMENT

Fortunately, the clothing and equipment needed for soccer is not expensive—or perhaps I should say that it need not be expensive. If you are playing for a team it is probable that your jersey, at least, will be supplied. For practice, a T-shirt makes a very acceptable jersey and any shorts will do, but whether you are practicing or playing "for real," you do need a good, well-fitting, and comfortable pair of football boots, or shoes. That is not to say that you cannot practice in a pair of tennis shoes—many professionals do so when the ground is hard—but you need a good pair of boots for match play and you need to wear them in practice so that they become as comfortable as a glove.

For a boy, I would always recommend boots, which are made slightly higher in the ankle than are the low-cut shoes. Any footballer has four joints which are constantly under strain during play—his knees and his ankles. There is not a lot that anyone can do to protect the knee from strain when playing games (knee injuries tend to be the result of bad luck as much as anything), but while the bones are still growing, ankles should be supported as much as possible to help prevent injury. A boot that gives some support to the ankle is therefore much better for boys than is the low-cut shoe. A bad ankle injury to a boy can finish him as a games player for the rest of his life, and so it is simply foolish to take unnecessary risks.

Much the same reasoning applies to the wearing of shin guards. Why risk a bad bruising, or worse, when there is a perfectly good and simple piece of equipment designed to protect you? Shin guards, these days, are light and comfortable to wear, and they are designed to protect you. If you want to be a soccer player, or a footballer of any kind, your legs are your most valuable asset—so look after them.

Soccer balls are obtainable in different materials, including leather, various plastics and laminates. For practice, it does not really matter which type of ball you use, provided it is the correct size and weight. For players up to the age of ten years, size three is recommended, and the ball should weigh eleven and one-half ounces. Players over the age of ten should use a size four ball, weighing twelve and one-half ounces. Any practice, done with any ball, is good practice, however, and many of today's star players learned most of their individual skills as youngsters, using old tennis balls, or, indeed, any ball they could find.

The Practice Grid

In Britain, where soccer is on the curriculum of almost all schools with pupils over the age of seven years, many schools and soccer clubs use a practice grid. This is sometimes marked out on grass, but more often on a hard surface—an asphalted school yard or something similar. The hard surface is more popular since the lines can be painted and will remain visible and usable for long periods, and since the surface is unaffected by weather, except for snow and ice. The great benefit of a practice grid is that a large number of players can practice the same, or different, skills within a limited area. This makes it easier for the teacher or coach to keep contact with the whole group while being able to give help to individuals where needed. As far as the players are concerned, each small group is working within a small area (10 yds x 10 yds) with clearly defined boundary lines, and this makes it necessary to use greater control, which makes them better players. The whole grid can be subdivided to make fields for small games, such as four against four.

Typical layouts for a practice grid are:

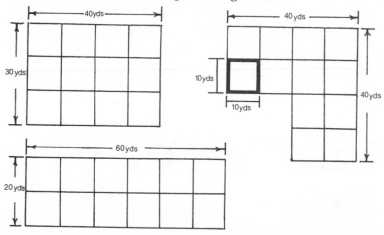

Each contains twelve squares, 10 yds x 10 yds, and the type of layout depends upon the shape of the space available. Each square is large enough for use by three or four players engaged in the type of game which helps them to master the basic skills, such as "Two on one," "Three on one," "Poison!" "Number passing," and numerous others.

It might be difficult to find such a grid in which to practice, but it is always a good idea to use a marked space of about eighty-five square yards in area. It need not be square—an oblong or even a circle will do—provided it has clearly marked boundaries. Although soccer is played on a fairly large field, you will find that, in a game, when you have got the ball, the area within which you have to do what you want to do is fairly small—you haven't got a lot of space to work in, because opponents are trying to crowd in on you. It is, therefore, very wise to learn to work in the sort of restricted area that a practice square provides, and it does not really matter what shape it is. The practice grid uses squares only because it is more convenient to site and easier to mark that way.

Passing and Dribbling

One of the special points to remember about soccer is that, except for the goalkeeper, everybody has to be able to do everything. There are no specialist kickers, specialist headers, or specialist runners—every player must be master of all the skills. The most frequently used skill is kicking, and so that is the one to start with. When kicking a ball, the object is to make it do exactly what you want it to do, to go where you want it to go. Not approximately where you want it to go, but *exactly* where you want it to go. Until you can make the ball do this, there is no point in thinking about how far you can kick it or how hard. Accuracy is everything. I was once told that a good games player (of any game) was one who "does the right thing quickly," and that seems to be a very good definition. In soccer no player can do the right thing, either quickly or slowly, until he can make the ball go where he wants it to go.

It is unfortunate that the English language does not

Fig. 1

have another word for the action of propelling a soccer ball with the foot, because the word "kicking" suggests a hard, sharp, leg-swinging action. Indeed, in all other types of football, such as American or Rugby, the ball *is* kicked with a hard, sharp, leg-swinging action, but this is not the most commonly used kick in soccer. In soccer the ball is *pushed* with the foot or *rolled* with the foot most of the time, because absolute accuracy is necessary. By pushing the ball with the foot, rather than kicking it in the normal way, we can learn to make it go where we want it to go.

PASSING WITH THE INSIDE OF THE FOOT

The ball can be pushed with either the inside of the foot as shown in figure 2, or with the outside border, but since the inside border is more often used and is easier to manipulate, we'll look at that first.

Whenever you are going to push a soccer ball, you use one foot to push it and the other foot to aim. Notice in figure 3 how the player's right foot is pointing at the other player, which is where he wants the ball to go. He is using the right foot as an aiming foot while he pushes the ball with the left.

Remember that you should practice pushing the ball with either foot. You must become as good a passer with your left foot as with your right.

To learn to pass with the inside of the foot, play the following game with a partner.

Fig. 2

Fig. 3

Poison!

This should be played by two boys. Later, the number of participants can be increased to three.

Boy No. 1 pushes the ball to boy No. 2. As soon as the ball leaves his foot, the ground he is standing on becomes POISON! He must *quickly* move at least five paces away from it. It doesn't matter whether he goes forward, backward, or sideways—as long as he moves quickly. Boy No. 2 receives the ball and pushes it to No. 1. As the ball leaves

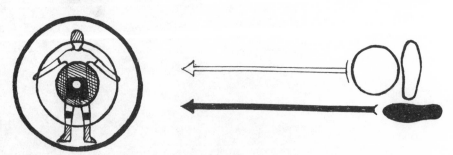

No. 2's foot the ground he is standing on becomes POISON! and he must in turn move away quickly. Both players must pass and move, pass and move, pass and move, until they have made twenty consecutive passes. Remember, every time the ball leaves your foot, the ground you are standing on becomes POISON! (See fig. 4.)

Points to remember:

1. Before pushing the ball to your partner, take aim by pointing the other foot at him (fig. 3).
2. As the ball comes to you, you must do two things. First, stop the ball with your foot, and then *look* for your partner before trying to push it back to him. Remember—as soon as you have the ball under your control, *look*.

Now that you are starting to push the ball around, let us look at the way you should be doing it.

When pushing with the inside of the foot you should:

1. Look at the ball all the time, which means that you must keep your head down while you are making the push. If you know anyone who plays golf, ask that person to explain about why it is important to keep the head down when striking the ball.
2. Point your nonkicking foot at the exact spot where you want the ball to go.

Fig. 4 Playing "Poison."—both players on the move

3. Turn your kicking foot fully sideways so that the whole of the inside border of the foot is presented to the ball.

4. Use a pushing action with the foot, to roll the ball where you want it to go.

5. As the ball goes away from you, keep the kicking foot moving after the ball. This is called "follow-through" and the same action is used in all games where a ball is struck, such as golf, tennis, baseball, hockey, and so on.

Each time you play the ball this way you should say to yourself, "Head down, push, follow through," until it becomes such a habit that you cannot do it any other way (figs. 5, 6, and 7).

Fig. 5 Passing with the inside of the foot—a last look at where he wants the ball to go

Fig. 6 Passing with the inside of the foot—head down

Fig. 7 Passing with the inside of the foot—follow through with the kicking leg—and the head still down!

6. Throughout the whole action, you should hold your arms out to the side to assist your balance. This is very important because, if you think about it, whenever you kick anything you are standing on one foot to do so. Therefore, whenever you kick, you are in a very delicate balancing situation, and need all the assistance you are able to get. Holding your arms out sideways helps a great deal.

PASSING WITH THE OUTSIDE OF THE FOOT

There will be times (and as you have gone through the practices, you will have noticed this) when, for one reason or another, it is not possible to play the ball with the inside of the foot. Sometimes it will take too long to get yourself into the right position to do so. On these occasions, you can play the ball with the outside border of the foot. Let us look at the technique of pushing with the outside of the foot.

The foot is held fairly rigidly and extended (pointed) so that it is firm when contact with the ball is made. The action is still a firm push, not a flick. It is a great temptation to flick the ball with the outside of the foot, but you must not do it, because a flick cannot be well directed and will not send the ball very far. The ball must be pushed firmly, and to do so requires that you make contact with the ball, using the base of the small toe, with a firm and rigid foot. Do not forget to follow through after the ball has left the foot (fig. 8).

Fig. 8

Remember, keep your head down so that you can watch the ball throughout the movement. Push the ball firmly with the outside edge of the foot and let the leg follow through as the ball moves.

Every soccer player should practice until he is an accurate passer of the ball with both the inside and the outside of the foot, either "first time" (as it comes to you, without stopping it first) or after having stopped the ball. Sometimes, however, it is necessary to move with the ball in your possession before passing. In soccer, this is called "dribbling," as it is in basketball, hockey, and other games.

DRIBBLING

One of the things coaches often say about a young soccer player is: "As soon as he gets the ball he becomes blind." What they mean is that the youngster has not learned to control a ball with confidence and consequently, when he has the ball at his feet, he dare not take his eyes off it. He drops his head to watch the ball closely, and then has no idea what is going on around him. There might be a teammate well placed to receive a pass, or there might be a good opportunity to shoot at goal, but he will not see it; he is "blind."

A good soccer player dribbles in the same way as a good basketball player, looking around him all the time (fig. 9). He can see the ball all right; he has trained himself to keep his eye on the ball while looking more or less straight ahead, keeping much of the game scene within the range of his vision. The really great players are able to do this even when they are under great pressure—with an opponent about to tackle.

The young soccer player must practice hard in order to perfect this ability, which can make the difference between a good player and a great player. When you are

Fig. 9 Dribbling with the insides of the feet and looking around

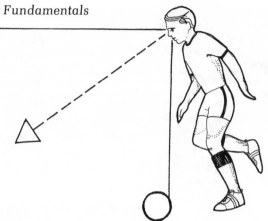

practicing, then, keep saying to yourself, "Look around, look around, look around." When you are practicing with others, say it to one another, and every teacher or coach should be urging his players to look around constantly.

The easiest, most basic way to dribble a soccer ball is to walk along pushing the ball from one foot to the other, using the inside of the foot all the time (fig. 9). If you do this, the path of the ball will be as below. As you can see,

this is a fairly slow way of going forward because the ball is constantly going back and forth across the player's line of progress. Sometimes you need to dribble slowly, and in that case you would move at a walk or slow run, but more often the player will need to move a bit faster with the ball. To move more quickly he will be pushing the ball *forward* with the inside of his foot, rather than *across* the line to his other foot. When he makes his next contact he will again push the ball forward with the inside of whichever foot is more convenient, as shown in the following illustration.

Dribbling in this way, with the inside of the foot, requires a lot of practice. This is the method of dribbling that gives you the most control over the moving ball, and at the same time allows you the greatest opportunity to look around. It cannot be said too often that the skill of *looking* while dribbling is as much a habit as anything else, and it is a habit you must acquire.

Unfortunately, once you start trying to move fast with the ball at your feet, you will find that you cannot be sure of making contact every time with the inside of the foot. You might wish to change direction, or your position might make it difficult to get the inside of your foot to the ball and still be able to do what you want to do. This means that sometimes you will have to play the ball with the outside of your foot. Every young player must be able to dribble by occasionally alternating between the inside and the outside of the foot—and that means the right and left foot, not just one—while keeping his head up to look around him (fig. 10).

The golden rule of all dribbling is to keep the ball close to the foot—to pretend that the ball is attached to your toes by a piece of elastic. If you let it get too far away from your foot a defender can come in and take it from you. On the other hand, the best way to fool a defender is to make him *think* that you have allowed the ball to get too far away from you when in fact you can play it with your foot at any time you choose. The defender, thinking that you have lost control, will come lunging in at the ball, and you will simply reach out a foot and pull it away from him, leaving him floundering, waving his leg at nothing.

While you are practicing, learn to judge how far ahead you can allow the ball to go and still be able to play it with

Fig. 10 *Dribbling fast—and still looking around!*

good control. This does not mean a distance at which you are still able to push a foot forward and stab the ball in any direction; it means to play the ball with *control*, either to continue the dribble or to make a good pass, or shot, or even to put your foot on it and stop it or pull it back.

Practice drills that are useful for learning dribbling are:

1. On your own, just dribbling the ball—anywhere. Concentrate on (a) keeping the ball close to your feet, and (b) keeping your head up so that you can look around you. You do not necessarily need a soccer ball to do this— almost any round ball will do. In Europe, many boys teach

themselves to dribble well by using an old tennis ball.

2. Set up a slalom course and dribble around it—either on your own, or as a member of a group of two or more.

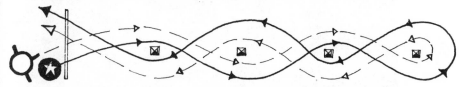

3. Relay races. In teams. From a starting line, dribble the ball up the course, around the marker and return. Stop the ball on the line; the next player carries on. A relay race could also be organized along a slalom course.

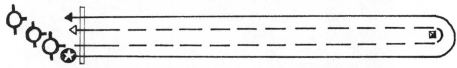

DRIBBLING AND PASSING GAMES

These games are ideal for small groups and fit well into the squares of a practice grid. They provide plenty of practice in the two types of push pass and they also give you the opportunity to use other passing techniques—the prod with the toe end (fig. 11) and even the back of the heel (fig. 12). These are not skills that you need to use very often, but you can learn how to use them in these games, as the opportunities arise.

Number Passing—Stage 1

Played by any number from three to six. It's easier to learn to play this game with four players, increasing the number of players as you become more familiar with the game.

Each player has a number, i.e. "Two," "Three," "Four," and "Five" (fig. 13). There is no No. 1 since, in soccer, 1 is the goalkeeper's number.

Fig. 11

Fig. 12

Fig. 13 *Number Passing, No. 2 has called for the ball and is moving in toward the passer (No. 5). No. 3 is changing direction to be ready to call for a pass from No. 2.*

No. 2 starts dribbling the ball, keeping on the move and in possession of the ball until No. 3 calls out his own number, "Three!" As soon as No. 3 does so, No. 2 passes the ball to him. No. 3 continues to dribble until No. 4 calls *his* own number, "Four!" Then No. 3 passes the ball to No. 4. No. 4 continues to dribble until No. 5 calls *his* own number, i.e. "Five!", when No. 4 passes the ball to No. 5. The game goes on with each player calling his own number when it is his turn to receive the ball and he is ready to receive it. No. 5 would pass to No. 2 and the sequence would start over.

Points to remember:

1. Do not pass the ball until the next number calls for it. Just keep dribbling if he doesn't call. Keep it—he'll soon get the message! By keeping the ball you are forcing him to move into a position to receive a pass.

2. As soon as you get the ball and start dribbling, *look* for the next number so that you are ready to push the ball to him as soon as he calls his number.

3. When it is your turn to call your number, start moving toward the boy with the ball as you call, so that you can receive the ball from a short pass rather than from a long one.

4. Watch the play so that you are ready to receive the ball as soon as the number before you gets it. As he calls his number, you should be moving toward him and calling your own number. This will keep the ball moving around quickly and teach everyone to react at a moment's notice.

Number Passing—Stage 2

Next, the same game is played in silence. The player who has the ball must watch for the next number moving into position to receive the ball, and then push it to him. Similarly the next number after him must move into position to receive the next pass. By now, having practiced Number Passing by calling numbers, every player will know who gives him the ball, and to whom he passes; for example, "Gary always gives me the ball and I always pass it to Chuck."

These two little games are very good for encouraging players to pass the ball quickly and accurately. The important things to learn from both these games are, first, that you must pass accurately. In a real match, if you pass well, your teammate will get the ball and your team will keep possession. If you do not pass accurately, your teammate will not get the ball—an opponent will nip in and take it, and then your team will have lost possession—and it will be your fault. The golden rule is that if you are in any doubt at all about whether your pass will reach a teammate, then don't make it—keep the ball at your feet until you *are* certain. The second thing you learn is that as soon as you have passed, you must move in order to keep yourself in the game. If you pass and then just stand where you are, you have taken yourself out of the game because the play has moved forward and you have not gone with it. Whenever you make a pass you must be sure that you are in position to have the ball passed back to you, and in order to be there, you've got to move as soon as you have made the pass.

We must now go on to learn how to use the push pass to beat an opponent.

Two Against One

Always remember this: In any team game, two must always beat one. If there are two of you against only one from the other team, the two of you *must* win. There is just no way that one has any chance of success against two, *provided that the two know what they are doing.* Once you understand this, you are well on the way to becoming a good team player, so we must now learn how to work a "two on one" situation to ensure success. Basically, there are four ways of working the situation, and they are:

1. the pass which goes "inside" the defender
2. the pass which goes "outside" the defender
3. the "wall" (or "1—2") pass
4. the continuous dribble, with the partner running as a decoy

It is absolutely necessary that every young soccer player learn to work the "two on one" situation almost automatically, so that as soon as he sees himself and a teammate in a "two against one" position he does the right thing quickly.

You set up practices for this by using an object as an opponent: a post, a chair, a barrel—almost anything (fig. 14).

Fig. 14 *Two against one—using a chair as an opponent*

You also have a goal of some sort—only about one yard wide—behind the object which is acting as the opponent, to allow you to finish the movement by scoring a goal, or by not scoring if you cannot push the ball accurately.

Note: In all the following practices, A1 and A2 are teammates trying to score a goal against 0, who is their opponent. Remember that, at this stage, 0 is an object, not a person.

shows the path of the player
shows the path of the ball
shows path of player with ball

SET MOVE No. 1

A1 dribbles the ball forward, going slightly to the right of 0. While still about 1.5 yards from 0, he pushes the ball across to A2, who dribbles on to score. Having passed the ball, A1 goes on past 0 and keeps level with A2, in case A2 needs to pass the ball back to him.

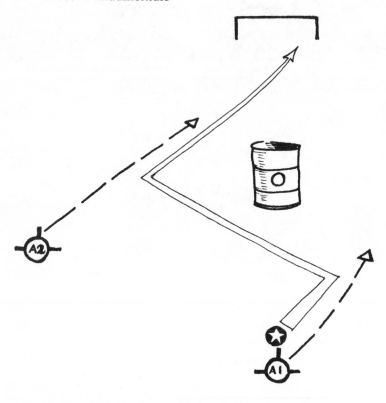

SET MOVE No. 2

A1 dribbles the ball forward, going slightly to the right of
0. While still 1.5 yards from 0, he pushes the ball behind
the back of 0. As he does so, A2 runs behind the back of 0 to
meet the ball, dribbles on and scores. As soon as he has
passed the ball A1 cuts left, across the front of 0 and then
runs for goal, to support A2, as he did in No. 1.

Note: In both the set moves, 1 and 2, it is important
that A2 not start to move forward until A1 pushes the ball.
He must not go past 0 until A1 has made the pass. This
means that A1 has got to push the ball at just the right
speed, and that A2 has got to move like a blue streak as
soon as A1 makes the push pass.

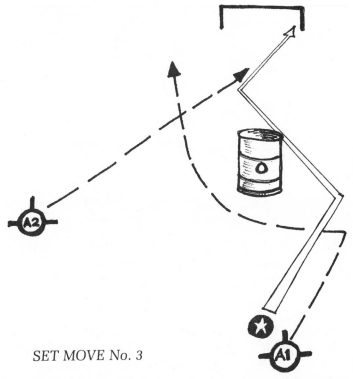

SET MOVE No. 3

A1 dribbles the ball toward 0, going slightly to the right a little faster than before. While still 1.5 yards from 0, A1 pushes the ball to A2 who, without any dribbling at all, immediately pushes it back into the space behind 0. As soon as A2 pushes the pass, A1 runs past 0 to receive the ball from A2, dribble on, and score. A2, having made the pass, runs toward goal to support A1. This move is called the "wall pass."

These three set moves should be practiced over and over. A2 should sometimes be on the left, as shown in the diagrams, and sometimes on the right, to make the move go in the other direction. A1 and A2 should swap places regularly. These drills should be continued until a score results every time a move is played. At that point we can introduce a live opponent. When a team is practicing these "two on one" moves, the coach will often act as the oppo-

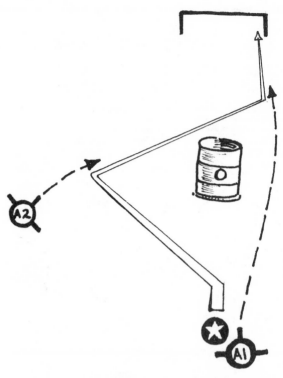

nent, because in this position he can direct the plays. He can also see what his players are doing well, and what they are not doing well, and correct where necessary. So we now put another player into the game, to be 0—the opponent.

You might have wondered why, at the beginning of each move, A1 goes to the right of 0. The reason is to make 0 move sideways, away from A2. 0 has to move, whether he wants to or not, since he must cover the man with the ball (A1), and try to keep between him and the goal. Once A1 has got 0 moving sideways, he can push the ball across to A2, knowing that 0 cannot stop, turn, run and get to A2. A1 has in fact, done two good things. He has first "pulled" the opponent away from A2 by making him go sideways, and then he has given A2 a good pass with plenty of room to work in.

Let us now see what to do if 0 decides that he is tired of being "pulled" sideways and that, instead, he will stay between A1 and A2 to try to cover both of them.

MOVE No. 4

Note: This is not a *set* move, since you cannot *make* it
happen. You make this move *when* 0 refuses to be
"pulled" and stays between you and your partner.

A1 dribbles the ball forward and to the right of 0. 0
thinks, "He is trying to pull me away from A2 again, so that
he can make a pass to him. I'm staying where I am, between
the two of them." Seeing that 0 will not come to him, A1
pushes the ball past 0, runs on, and scores.

A2 can help by running on and getting ahead of 0,
which will probably make 0 half turn toward A2 to see
what he is doing, thus giving A1 a clearer run to the ball. In
this case, A2 is acting as a decoy runner.

While playing in all these practices, you should try
hard to push the ball with either foot. Everybody has a

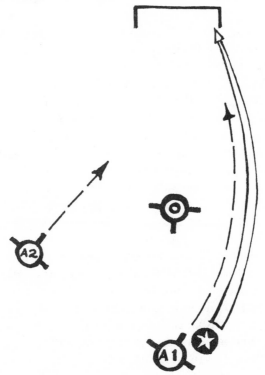

strong foot and a weak one, and if you want to be a good
soccer player, you must educate your weak foot along with
your strong one. It will be very difficult at first—the weak
foot will just not do what you want it to—but if you keep
practicing it will get better and better, until you are the
complete "two-footed" player.

Two Against One, With A Live Opponent

One of the really important things that you must understand, and must learn to do when you are playing, either in
practice or in games, is to make the defender commit
himself. This is sometimes called "attacking" the defender.

When you have the ball, and there is a defender in a
position to stop your progress, there are really only two
choices open to you.

You may either beat him with a pass, or beat him
yourself by taking the ball past him. Whichever you
choose to do, you first have to make the defender think that
you are going to do something else, and make him move to
stop your doing it. If a player with the ball allows a defender to stand and wait for him to arrive with the ball, he is
giving all the advantage to the defender. The defender can
wait, perfectly balanced and ready to move either way.
Consequently, the attacker must try to make the defender
move in the way he wants him to move. Using the same set
plays as before, with a live "0" (opponent), let us see how
we can force him to move.

As an example, in this diagram, the attacker, A1, is
going forward with the ball but is also moving to the right.
This makes the defender 0 move across to the right in order
to keep between A1 and the goal. A1 has now forced 0 to
move—he has made him commit himself to going across
to the right. 0 probably does not want to go to the right. He
has probably seen A2 on the other side of him and would
much rather stay in the middle to keep an eye on both of

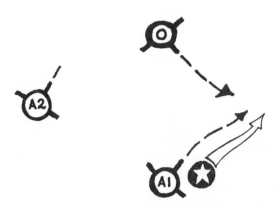

them, but he *cannot*. A1, who has the ball and is therefore the danger man, has started on a run which will take him around the outside of 0 to the goal. Whether he wants to or not, 0 has got to move across to cut A1 off from the goal.

A1 has now:

1. "pulled" 0 right away from A2, so that if he wants to push the ball into the space in front of A2, 0 cannot stop A2 going in on goal with the ball, and;
2. got 0 moving to the right, so that if A1 decides to cut back to the left with the ball, 0 now has to stop and turn and start moving the other way in order to try to stop him. By the time 0 has done all this, A1 and the ball should be long gone!

In short, what A1 has done is to force 0 into a bad defensive position by making him move out to the right.

If, on the other hand, A1 merely came straight forward with the ball, all 0 would have to do would be to let him come to within about 2 yards of him and then start backing away, keeping between A1 and the goal, and, at the same time, keeping an eye on A2. As he backs away, 0 is

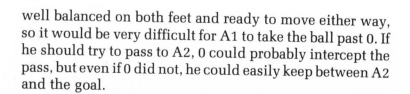

well balanced on both feet and ready to move either way, so it would be very difficult for A1 to take the ball past 0. If he should try to pass to A2, 0 could probably intercept the pass, but even if 0 did not, he could easily keep between A2 and the goal.

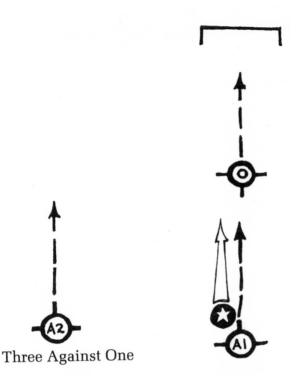

Three Against One

When you are playing "two on one" games and you have the ball, decisions about what to do are fairly easy, because there is only one person you *can* pass the ball to, and that is your partner. All you have to do is watch what the opponent is doing, and as soon as your partner has moved clear of him, push the ball to your partner. If, however, there are three of you against one, you not only have to make the opponent commit himself, you also have to decide which of your two teammates is better placed to receive a pass. Again, you should start playing three against one in a square or some other marked space, where all you are trying to do is to keep the ball moving about between the three of you, without the opponent's getting it. (See fig. 15, where player No. 6 is the opponent.) Now that the boy with the ball must choose which of his partners to push the ball to, it becomes more difficult for him, especially if the opponent is close to him. It is at this point that young players should learn to call for the ball. Professional soccer players talk to one another all the time they are playing,

Fig. 15 Three against one. The defender, No. 6, is going in very aggressively on No. 2, who is already playing an easy pass off to No. 4. Nos. 2, 4, and 5 have all moved well to keep in a triangular formation and make life difficult for No. 6.

but it is a very disciplined sort of talking. Nobody says anything unless it is helpful to a teammate. When playing small games like "three on one" it does help the boy with the ball if his teammates let him know when they are ready to receive the ball (remember "number passing"). Sometimes the opponent will be guarding the boy with the ball so closely that the boy might not see the teammate who is best placed to receive the ball. In such a case the teammate must call for the ball. There are two golden rules in calling for the ball.

1. If you are in a good position to receive the ball, let the boy with the ball know this by calling *his* name—just the name, nothing else. If Chuck has the ball and you want it, you just call "Chuck." You don't say, "Over here, Chuck" or "Gimme the ball, Chuck"—you just call his name. And you call only *once*. When you've called, Chuck knows you are there and ready for the ball. If he doesn't give it to you, it is because he has other plans for it, and he doesn't want you yelling "Chuck, Chuck, Chuck, Chuck," at him. So, remember, just his name, and just once, and only when you are in a good position to receive the ball (fig. 16).

Fig. 16 The player is calling for the ball—letting his teammate know he is there, ready for a pass, and where he wants the ball delivered.

2. When you have the ball, if a teammate calls your name to let you know that he is in a good position to receive the ball, he means *now*. In five or ten seconds' time the position may have changed entirely and by that time he may not want the ball. So, when a teammate calls for the ball, unless you have positive plans to do something else, give it to him quickly. Pause only long enough to see where he wants the ball and then push it there.

When you are playing "three on one," it is best if the three players who are playing together try to form a triangle (and retain it) all the time they are playing. The general dimensions of the triangle will change, and so will

Fig. 17 Because they have not moved, 2 and 5 are close together, behind the defender (6) and 4 cannot get a pass to either of them.

the positions of the players in it, but the triangular shape should be kept. If it is kept, no matter where the defender positions himself, someone is in a position to receive a pass. (Look again at fig. 16.)

You should also remember what we did right at the start; pass and move still applies. As soon as you push the ball to a teammate, move. If all three of you move every time you make a pass, life becomes absolutely impossible for 0. If, however, you do not move when you've passed, all 0 has to do is to keep himself roughly in the middle of the triangle and wait for one of you to make a slightly bad pass, which he can then intercept (fig. 17). It is just like the situation in "two on one"—you must make the defender commit himself. You must not let him stay where he is, comfortable and balanced. He will not move unless you force him to do so.

Kicking

There will be occasions when you need to kick the ball with rather more force and speed than the push will produce. Shooting for goal might well be one such occasion. Hitting a long pass for defensive reasons might be another. In these situations a different type of kick must be used. You have perhaps noticed that I have used the term "hitting" in connection with this type of kick. It is a crisp, explosive type of action, in the same way that hitting a ball with a bat is a crisp, explosive action.

    Keeping the ball on the ground when hitting it in this way is a lot more difficult than when using a push—first because you will be using more force that you did with the pushing action, and then because kicking is a more difficult technique to master. There are four points to remember (fig. 18):

1. Put your nonkicking foot right next to the ball. If it is placed slightly behind the ball you will kick the ball into

Fig. 18

the air, because you will be leaning back as you make contact, allowing your kicking foot to slide under the ball. If your nonkicking foot is placed too far forward you will hit the ball downward into the ground, and it will rebound upward into the air.

2. The knee of the kicking leg should be immediately above the ball as contact is made.

3. The ball is struck with the upper surface of the foot—it is often said that the ball is kicked with the player's shoelaces—and this is a fairly accurate description of the point of contact. The toe of the boot is scraping the ground as the ball is hit.

4. Use a good, long follow-through of the kicking leg as the ball goes away. This makes for accuracy, always provided that the follow-through is in the direction of the target!

When hitting a ball in this way, bearing in mind that you want to keep the ball on the ground, you must remember to direct the kicking force into the middle or the upper half of the ball. This will help you avoid "getting under the ball" which always causes the ball to go into the air.

If, on the other hand, you *want* the ball to go into the air—maybe to make a long, defensive clearance kick or to pass the ball to a teammate's head—then a slightly different technique is used. Goalkeepers use this technique when making a goal kick; wingers use it when making corner kicks, and almost every player who makes a free kick uses it. This is, then, the type of kick that every member of the team should practice.

1. The nonkicking foot is placed beside and slightly behind of the ball.
2. The contact point is the top of the foot, but slightly to the inside—that is, the inner line of lace holes on your boot or shoe.
3. The foot should make contact with the ball at a point slightly below the midline. This in itself will cause the ball to rise.

4. Again, a good, long follow-through with the kicking foot in the direction of the target is important. Because your body is leaning slightly back as you hit the ball, the follow-through can and should be fuller than it was when you were hitting the low ball.

If you use this technique, but aim to stab the foot under the ball and stop the foot as soon as contact is made—no follow-through—you will "chip" the ball. The ball will go high, but only for a short distance, and as it drops to the ground will almost stop instead of bouncing and rolling on as it normally would. As the foot goes under the ball to make contact, it puts a backspin on it—in the same way that a similar action would apply backspin in tennis, table tennis, or golf. The chip is a very useful skill to acquire and is used for putting the ball over the head of an advancing goalkeeper to score, or for passing over the head of a player to a teammate.

THE VOLLEY

Sometimes it will be necessary to move in and kick a ball that is in the air. As in tennis, this is called a volley, and the difficult thing about it is that you cannot choose either the position of the ball or the position of your body when such a kick has to be made. If you had any choice you would probably wait for the ball to drop to the ground and then push it or hit it as you have done up to now. When an

Fig. 19

Fig. 20

opponent is moving in on you, however, he will get to the ball first and steal it, if you don't move in and play the ball. You have no choice—you must move in and kick the ball while it is still in the air, before he does. Again, you might want to make a quick pass or a shot at goal, and you cannot wait for the ball to drop before making your move. Under these circumstances you should go in and volley the ball. You should let the ball drop as low as possible before kicking it—the higher it is the more difficult the kick— and you must, as always, watch the ball constantly. You should meet the ball with the top of your foot (your shoelace) if you want a strong kick that will travel a long way (fig. 19), or with the inside border of the foot if you want to make a short pass (fig. 20). The body should be leaning back slightly as you make contact with the ball.

The overhead volley, known as the "bicycle kick," is a very useful skill to possess. It is especially valuable to a striker who often has half a chance to volley the ball while standing with his back to the goal. The ability to shoot at goal using an overhead volley will often bring a score, if only because none of the defenders is expecting it to happen. Use the following technique:

1. Watch the ball carefully as it comes to you, lean back and allow yourself to start to fall backward.
2. As you start to fall, still watching the ball, swing the kicking leg up to "hook" the ball back over the head.

It is possible to do this, as described, and keep the non-kicking foot on the ground, which allows you to break your fall (fig. 21). Done this way, however, the resulting volley will not be powerful and the ball will tend to rise. To hit a powerful overhead volley which will not rise, the player must jump in order to lift his hips high. Since he is falling backward as he jumps, he must "scissor kick" his legs, kicking the ball with the "second" leg. Once the player has jumped, both feet are off the ground and he has no means of breaking his fall. Consequently, this is one skill that should not be practiced too frequently.

Fig. 21

BENDING OR SWERVING THE BALL ("THE BANANA KICK")

Strangely enough, kicks which result in the ball's swerving in flight more often occur accidentally than deliberately. For this reason, the ball frequently misses its mark. In order to kick the ball along a straight line, which is what we want to do most of the time, the foot should touch the ball at the vertical center line of the ball.

If contact is made to one side of the center line, the ball will spin and swerve, whether on the ground or in flight. This is exactly what happens when a ball is sliced or pulled in golf or tennis—it has been struck off center. A good player, however, learns to make the ball swerve deliberately. Any player who takes a corner kick should be able to make the ball swerve, either inward toward the goal (the inswinger) or outward, away from the goal (the outswinger). A player taking a free kick within scoring distance of the goal always finds a wall of opponents lined up 10 yards in front of him, almost completely blocking the goal. The goalie will have the rest of the goal covered. It is, therefore, very useful to be able to "bend" the ball around the end of the "wall." Many goals are scored this way. Basically, the technique is one of hitting the ball to the side of the center line of the ball. If the contact is to the left of center, the ball will swerve to the right, and if the contact is to the right of center the ball will swerve to the left. If the foot is traveling across the face of the ball as contact is made, the swerve will be more pronounced.

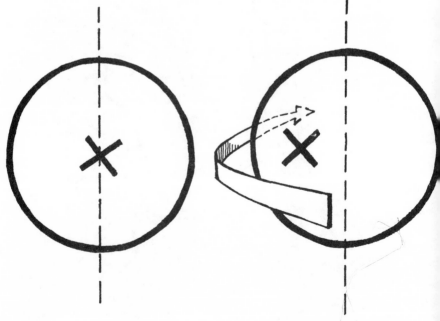

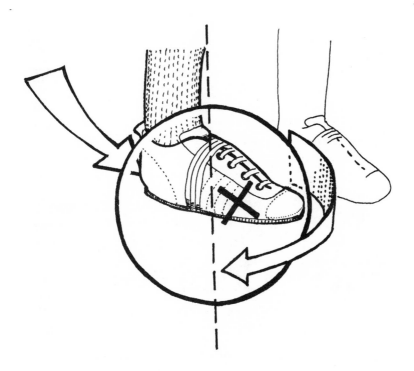

Ball Control

Every soccer player needs to be able to bring the ball quickly under his control as it comes to him and then to be able to move efficiently. Controlling the ball as you receive it is generally known as "trapping" because you are making a trap out of some part of your body (other than your hands) and catching the ball in it.

On many occasions you will want to bring the ball under control, slowing its pace, without "killing" or stopping it. This can be done with the foot, when the ball is coming along the ground to you, by executing the reverse action of the push pass with the inside of the foot. You must position yourself so that the ball is coming straight at you, making sure that the other foot—the one that you are not going to use to meet the ball—is pointed straight at the ball. Turn the foot outward and push it forward so that you meet the ball with the inside border of the foot. As contact is made, start to withdraw the foot straight back, with the

Fig. 22

leg relaxed. This cushions the impact, absorbing the ball's force. By the time the ball is level with the other foot, it should be almost stationary, fully under your control and ready for you to play in whichever way you choose (fig. 22).

A similar technique is used to deal with a ball that is coming toward you but is bouncing at about knee height. You prepare to meet the ball in the same way, except that you lift the foot and do not extend it so far forward—you do not reach out for the ball. Instead, you plan to meet the ball when it is level with the other leg, or thereabouts. You then withdraw the foot, as before, to take the pace off the ball (fig. 23).

Fig.

WITH THE CHEST

A ball which is bouncing high, or coming straight toward you at chest height, or which is dropping from a low height, can be controlled by letting it come onto your chest. As contact is made, the chest and stomach are pulled back, the arms lifted sideways and the upper body bent forward, so that a curved surface is presented to the ball. When the ball hits this curved surface, it will drop straight down to the feet, where it can be played off, or further controlled with the feet (fig. 24).

Fig. 24

If the ball is dropping from a height, it is often better to use the chest as a platform on which the ball can bounce before it drops to the feet. As the ball drops, the whole of the upper part of the body is arched sharply backward. At the same time, the arms are raised sideways, both for balance and to flatten the platform formed by the chest (fig. 25). The ball is allowed to drop onto the chest and the upper body gives slightly as contact is made. The ball then bounces gently on the chest and rolls down the front of the body to the feet.

Fig. 25

WITH THE THIGH

A steeply dropping ball may also be brought under control by using the thigh in much the same way as the chest was used in the platform method. The thigh should be lifted until it is parallel with the ground. As the ball drops onto it, the thigh is lowered slightly to take the speed off the ball (fig. 26). The ball is then allowed to drop to the ground.

One of the best practices to help you to acquire this kind of ball control is an individual drill where you merely try to keep the ball in the air. You toss the ball up and then play it with your head, chest, thighs and feet, trying to keep it off the ground as long as possible. If it does drop to the ground, then flick it up with your foot and continue. This can also be done against a wall, keeping the ball off the ground while using rebounds off the wall.

Remember that you have *two* feet and *two* thighs and you must learn to use both. You should spend more time practicing with your weak foot than with your strong one. Professional soccer players or coaches will often say of a poor player, "The only thing his left foot is good for is standing on."

SHIELDING

A very important skill that all young players should acquire and practice as they learn to control and dribble a ball is shielding. You will read elsewhere in this book that the best time for a defender to make a tackle is at the moment that the attacker is trying to get the ball under control. The attacker cannot really concentrate on both controlling the ball and avoiding a tackle at the same time, and is an easy target for the tackler.

To avoid losing the ball before you've really got it, shield the ball with your body by placing your body be-

Fig. 26

tween the ball and the opponent who wants to take it from
you. The defender will not be able to reach the ball because
your legs will be in his way—between him and the ball. As

you can see in figure 27, if a player is shielding the ball with his body, it is impossible for the defender to make a tackle without committing a foul.

As a general rule, then, try to keep your body between your opponent and the ball when an opponent is in a position to challenge for it.

Fig. 27

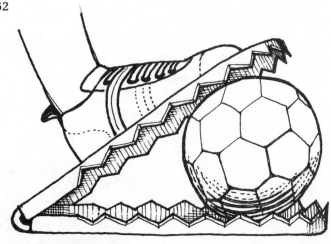

TRAPPING

Catching the ball between your foot and the ground is the only true "trap." This may be done with the sole of the foot, with the inside, or the outside of the foot. Once the ball is in the trap, the top jaw—your foot—closes gently, but firmly, and holds it. As soon as the ball is in the trap, however, the foot must draw back very, very slightly. This ensures that the ball stays in the trap and does not bounce out again, as it will if the foot is held too rigidly.

With The Sole Of The Foot

Watch the ball carefully as it comes toward you. Lift your foot off the ground and point your toes upward. You should now have positioned yourself so that the ball will hit the ground under your trapping foot. As it does so, press the foot down onto it (fig. 28). Having trapped the ball, *look up* and move away with the ball. Trapping the ball under the sole of the foot "kills" it absolutely and you will be left with a "dead ball" under your foot, unless you begin moving away with the ball immediately. This is why

Fig. 28

you should always make sure that there are no opponents running toward you before you go about trapping a ball in this way. During the time it takes you to trap the ball and then get on the move again, you are a sitting target for an opponent.

With The Inside Of The Foot

This is used when you are standing sideways along the line of the ball's trajectory. The trap is made between the ground and the inside border of the foot—along most of its

Fig. 29

length and nearly as far up as the ankle. Once again, watch the ball as it comes to you. The ball hits the ground and the trapping part of the foot at the same time (fig. 29). The foot is pressed onto the ball and then relaxed to avoid presenting a rigid surface, which would cause the ball to bounce out of the trap. Although the ball is held in the trap, this action does not "kill" it absolutely. It can be pushed forward with the inside of the foot to make a pass or start a dribble. Thus, when trapping with the inside of the foot, you can capture the ball and start to move away with it almost in one continuous action. Don't forget to *look up* as you start to move away.

With The Outside Of The Foot

This is used when you want to move away from your position *immediately* after trapping the ball. It may be that you have an opponent coming at you; it may be that you want to turn and go in a different direction; whatever the reason, you need to trap the ball and be on your way immediately. Watch the ball as it comes toward you and make the trap between the outside border of the foot and ankle, and the ground. The trapping foot is turned well outward and, as before, is pressed down onto the ball as the ball hits the ground (fig. 30). As the trap is made, the foot is

Fig. 30

relaxed to prevent its rebounding away from you, but the ball can now be pushed with the outside of the foot so that you move away with the ball *as* you trap it. As soon as you feel that you have successfully trapped the ball, lift your head and *look around* as you push the ball to start moving away.

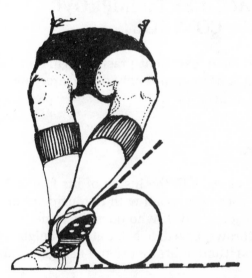

Basically, then, there are three important things which must be practiced until they become automatic:

1. Watch the ball right into the trap. (This will cause you to lower your head.)
2. Capture the ball in the trap. (Your head will stay down as you make sure that you've got it.)
3. Lift your head to look around you, and make your next move—pass, dribble, shoot, or whatever.

Every other player knows that you are a sitting target while you are trapping a ball, because you've got to stop—even if only momentarily—in order to do it, and because you have to concentrate on watching the ball. For that moment you are stationary *and* blind, which is just how an opponent wants you. Therefore, you should practice until you can trap smoothly and quickly, no matter how the ball comes to you.

PRACTICES TO IMPROVE BALL CONTROL

There are many excellent practice drills for ball control which are done in groups of two and three, and which can be varied as necessary.

In Pairs

1. No. 1 passes with the inside of his foot to No. 2, who takes the pace off the ball with the inside of this foot and passes it back to No. 1, who does the same.
2. No. 1 throws the ball to No. 2 at knee height. No. 2 takes the pace off it and returns it to No. 1 using the outside of his foot.
3. No. 1 throws the ball to No. 2 at chest height. No. 2 controls it with his chest and then passes it back to No. 1, who takes the pace off it with the inside of his foot.
4. No. 1 throws the ball high to No. 2, who lets it drop onto his chest and roll down. As it hits the ground he passes it back to No. 1 with the outside of his foot.
5. No. 1 throws the ball up and, as it drops, controls it with his thigh. He then passes it to No. 2, who passes it back to him, using a first-time pass with the inside of the foot.

In Triangular Formation

1. No. 1 passes to No. 2, who controls the ball with his foot, at the same time turning to shield the ball from No. 1.

No. 2 then passes to No. 3, who shields from No. 2 and passes to No. 1, who shields from No. 3 and passes to No. 2, and so on.

2. No. 1 throws the ball to No. 2, who traps it with the sole of his foot and then passes it off to No. 3, who takes the pace off the ball with his foot and passes it to No. 1, who stops it with the inside of his foot, picks it up and starts again.

3. No. 1 throws the ball to No. 2, who traps it with the outside of his foot and then passes it off to No. 3, who hits it for the first time to No. 1, using the outside of his foot.

4. No. 1 throws the ball to No. 2, varying the type of throw he uses. No. 2 traps the ball with either the sole, the inside, or the outside of the foot and then passes it off to No. 3, who hits a first-time pass to No. 1, using either the inside or the outside of the foot.

All these drills can be adapted to any skill that you want to work on. The important thing is to have every player doing something useful and not merely serving the ball to someone else.

Heading

FROM A STANDING POSITION

Heading is the part of soccer that is most frequently done badly. Some world-famous players readily admit that they cannot head a ball well. It is true that when playing in games, players in some positions—notably defenders and strikers—have to head the ball more frequently than players in other positions—for instance, wingers—but every player ought to be able to make the ball do what he wants it to do with his head as well as with his feet. Like every other skill, this is a matter of learning to do it properly, and then practicing until you can do it perfectly every time. The first thing you must learn is to "meet" the ball correctly, with your forehead. There is only a very small area on your head which is almost flat—and that is the central lower part of your forehead, the part used in heading.

If you imagine a rectangle drawn on your forehead, like this,

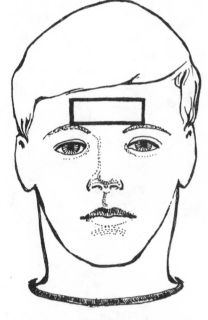

you have described the flat area of your forehead that should make contact with the ball.

Take a soccer ball in both hands, and hold it in front of your face, as shown in figure 31. The ball should be about six to eight inches away from your forehead. At the same time, push your forehead forward fast, simultaneously pulling the ball back toward your forehead. The ball will be headed forward out of your hands. Make sure that it is the contact area of the forehead that meets the ball, and make sure that you are watching the ball throughout— before you start the action, as you pull it toward you and move your head forward, and as it goes away.

When you first start heading, it is very tempting to close your eyes as your forehead makes contact with the ball. You, no doubt, expect hitting a ball with your head to be uncomfortable. This is a natural reflex—but there is no

Fig. 31

need! To head a ball well gives you one of those really nice feelings that you get from time to time in sport. When you hit a baseball just right, with that lovely crack of bat on ball, the feeling in your hands is marvelous. A really good smash in tennis gives you a similar sort of feeling, and so does heading a ball well. It is in no way uncomfortable—in fact, it feels great!

Now try heading the ball out of your hands by moving only your head. Do not pull the ball toward your head, just push your head. This will mean holding the ball closer to your head when you start—only four or five inches away. Again, keep watching that ball! You will be surprised how much force you can put into a header when you are holding the ball this way and meeting the ball correctly with the contact area of the forehead.

Now try throwing the ball up and heading it as it comes down. Don't throw it too high—a foot above head level is about right. This time, you should try to head the ball downward. When playing in a game, you will need to be able to head the ball upward, downward, and sideways, but the downward header is the one you will use most. Soccer is a game which is played mainly with the feet, and the feet are usually on the ground, so that is where the ball needs to be. Occasionally it gets up in the air and you have to head it, but most of the time you head it to get it back onto the ground, so you must practice that downward header.

Practice heading with a partner. Throw the ball up and head it to his feet. He then throws it up and heads it to your feet, and so on (fig. 32).

Practice against a wall. Throw the ball up, and head it down against the wall. Make a mark low down on the wall and try to hit it with the ball every time.

Fig. 32

You will notice, both from the photographs and from doing it yourself, that to add some force to your headers you will need to lean the whole top part of your body backward and then bring it forward as your head meets the ball. You are, in fact, using the whole of your body from the waist upward to get a good, forceful header (fig. 33).

You will need to watch the ball very carefully to ensure that it is in exactly the right place as you meet it

Fig. 33

with your forehead. If it is slightly too high, the round part of your head, above the contact area, will meet it, and it will go upward.

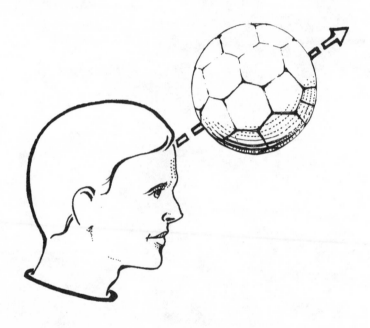

If it is slightly too low, some part of your face below the contact area (probably your nose!) will meet it, and the ball could go anywhere (and I promise you that you will not enjoy it very much!).

If, however, the correct contact area meets the ball, it will go exactly where you want it to go—in this case forward and downward.

You will also need to pay some attention to the positioning of your feet. In the first place, for the type of heading you are practicing now, both feet need to be firmly on the ground. This provides a solid base, and you need a solid base in order to get some force behind your heading.

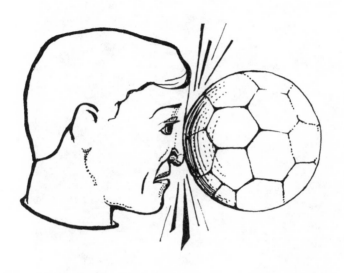

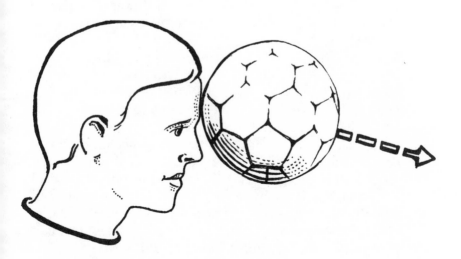

Fig. 34

It also puts you in a well-balanced position. Look again at the photographs and notice first how one foot is always ahead of the other. You need this for balance, because you are going to bring the top half of the body forward pretty forcefully. If you did this with the feet side by side, you would probably topple forward. Notice, also, that although the boy comes up onto his toes as he meets the ball and heads it forward, his feet do not leave the ground (fig. 34).

Once you have mastered the art of heading the ball downward, you should practice heading it straight forward, and heading it upward. Heading it straight forward is simple. You began your heading drills by heading a ball straight forward, out of your hands. All you have to do is to move your head straight forward and meet the middle part of the ball with the contact area (fig. 35).

Fig. 35

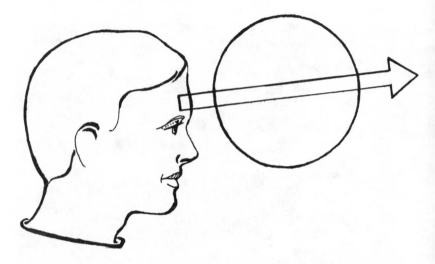

When you were heading it downward, you waited for the ball to drop slightly below forehead level and then moved your head forward and downward and met the ball with the contact area.

In order to head it upward, you meet the ball when it is still slightly above forehead level. Because the ball is above eye level, you will be holding your head back

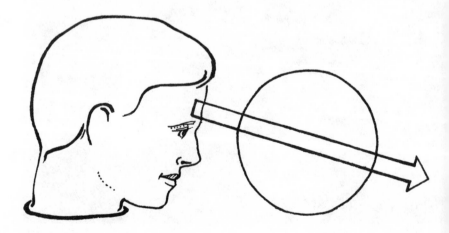

slightly in order to see it properly. The head, held slightly back, is moved forward to meet the ball with the contact area (fig. 36).

Fig. 36

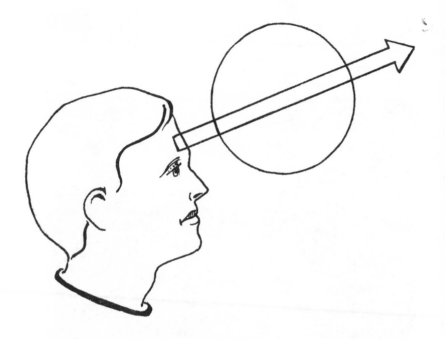

Practice this by throwing the ball up and heading it as it drops. Do this against a wall, or with a partner throwing the ball to you. Try to head it over something—a volleyball net or even a string stretched between two upright objects will do.

Until now, all the heading practice drills have been concerned with sending the ball forward, either straight forward, or upward or downward and forward. We must now learn to head the ball sideways. The ball needs to be coming at you from the front, and so it is better to have two or three in a group to practice this skill. What you are trying to do, when you first start on this drill, is merely to change the direction of a ball which is coming toward you. It is coming straight at you, and you are going to make it go to one side or the other. Accuracy is all important, but force does not matter at all here.

As you stand facing the ball, feet slightly apart, nicely balanced, you must follow the procedure below.

Assuming you wish to head the ball away to your right,

1. Sway your upper body to the left so that the ball is now going to pass to the right of your head.
2. Turn your head and upper body to the right and lean back so that the contact area of your forehead is aimed at the place you want the ball to go.
3. Push the upper part of the body and head at the ball as it comes level with the contact area (fig. 37).

Fig. 37

If there are three of you, No. 1 can throw the ball to No. 2, and No. 3 can collect it after No. 2 heads it; then No. 3 can throw it back to No. 2, who will head to No. 1.

You must be sure to watch the ball constantly until it touches your forehead, and keep watching it as it goes away to your target—in this case, another boy. You must also be sure that you meet the ball with the contact area, and not with the side of your head. If you do meet it with the side of your head, you have either not turned your head quickly enough, or far enough, or both. As a result, the ball will skid off the head. As you become more used to heading sideways, you will probably start moving your back foot around as you turn the upper part of your body, in order to bring your whole body around to face the target. This is perfectly natural, and will allow you to put more force behind your header because you've made your base more solid and you are better balanced.

It is important that you practice heading sideways both to the right and left. Once you are doing it well, practice the downward, upward, and forward motions. It is probable that more goals are scored by a sideways— downward header than with any other kind, and so this technique is very well worth a lot of practice time.

JUMPING TO HEAD THE BALL

It would be very nice if all heading could be done with both feet firmly on the ground, because, as you have found out, this is a well-balanced position. From such a solid base you can bring some real power to the header by using the whole of the upper body in the heading action. However, in a game of soccer, the ball sometimes reaches a height where a player has to jump in order to head it, and heading the ball in the air is a little different than heading with the feet on the ground. The main difference is that you cannot draw your trunk back while you are in the air without hopelessly disturbing your balance. When you are heading a ball in mid-jump it becomes mainly a matter of neck power rather than trunk power. The other techniques are exactly the same as they are for heading from a standing position. Obviously, the timing of the jump is very important. You want to meet the ball at the peak of your jump—not on your way up or down. Just as some of the great basketball players seem to have the ability to "hang in the air" at the top of their jump—to get up there

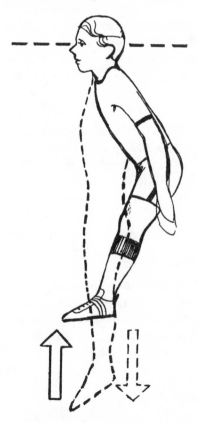

and then stay there while they take a leisurely shot at the basket—some soccer players seem to develop the same ability. This gives them plenty of time to direct their headers. The ability to do this—in either basketball or soccer—is no magical gift; it's all a matter of perfect timing. It is knowing how to do what you have to do—shoot or head a ball—right at the peak of the jump, plus the knowledge that if you push your trunk forward when you are at the top of the jump, it will give you more time at the top. When you jump upward, you bend at the ankles, knees, and hips as you take off, and, unless you make a real effort to do so, you never really straighten out at the hips as you go upward. If, at the top of your jump, you do make a real effort to push your hips forward, this effectively gives you another split second at the peak of your jump. It's well worth practicing.

When you come to think about it, in all the team running games—basketball, football of any description, field hockey and the like—about eighty percent of the qualities required to be a good player have nothing to do with the object you play with—the ball—but involve the most basic skills of human movement—the ability to run fast, start, stop, and turn quickly, jump high with good timing, and so on. Only twenty percent of the skills necessary to the athlete have to do with how well you can kick, dribble, shoot, or head a ball.

You should practice heading while in the air much as you did when you had your feet on the ground—with a partner to throw the ball up so that you can jump and head it sideways, downward, upward, or straight forward. Once you are up there, you need only to:

1. keep watching that ball, all the way to your forehead and then to its target, and
2. meet the ball with the contact area every time (fig. 38). If you meet it with the top or side of your head, you've timed your jump badly.

Fig. 38

When you jump to head a ball, think about your balance. With both feet off the ground this really *is* balance—the hard way! As soon as you are off the ground, try to straighten your legs and get them and your feet together. You have a fairly complicated movement to perform at the top of your jump if you are going to head that ball well, so you need to be well balanced, and you will not be well balanced if your legs are sticking out at odd angles.

PRACTICE DRILLS AND GAMES WHICH WILL IMPROVE HEADING

With A Partner

1. Hold the ball with two hands, and head it out of the hands to the partner (see page 72).
2. Throw the ball up and head it (a) straight to your partner, (b) to his feet, and (c) over him (heading upward).
3. Your partner throws the ball to your head; you head it (a) straight to him, (b) to his feet, and (c) over him.
4. Against a wall, first on your own, see how many consecutive headers you can make. Next, with your partner, alternate heading the ball against the wall, to see how many consecutive headers you can make between you.
5. Keep the ball up (a) on your own, and (b) with a partner, to see how many consecutive headers you can make.
6. Heading in the air, practice drills 2 and 3 with the ball thrown, so that a jump is necessary.

With A Larger Group

Practice sideways headings in a triangular formation. Player No. 1 throws the ball to No. 2, who heads it sideways to No. 3. Repeat with No. 3 throwing the ball to No. 2, who heads it sideways to No. 1.

Tackling

Tackling is one of the most difficult soccer skills to perform well. It is not only a matter of keeping an opponent from gaining ground with the ball, as it often is in football or basketball, but it is also a matter of taking the ball from him while obeying some fairly strict rules—the most important of which is to play the ball, not the opponent's body. Quite often, in playing the ball, you will make some contact with the opponent, but the referee must be satisfied that this contact was made as part of an attempt to play the ball. If he thinks that you intended to make bodily contact without bothering about the ball—or even if you make accidental contact during a failed attempt to play the ball—the referee must call a foul on you if your contact hinders the opponent in any way.

Certain deliberate contacts are permitted, provided that both the players involved are close enough to the ball to be able to play it. The shoulder charge, where one player does little more than nudge the shoulder of an opponent to shove him off balance, is often used in conjunction with a tackle and is perfectly fair. The important thing to understand about tackling is that you must not try to stop the man with the ball by attacking the man—your attack must be on the ball. A good tackle is one where the tackler emerges with the ball well under control at his feet.

Sometimes, a desperate tackle is necessary to take the ball from an opponent who would otherwise certainly score. At such times, you cannot afford to be too particular about what will happen to you or to the ball. You will probably end up on your back and the ball might go off the field altogether, but it does not matter; your tackle has stopped a score. These occasions are very rare, however. The first important thing to learn is how to tackle firmly, successfully, and with full control so that you come out of the tackle with the ball at your feet.

BLOCK TACKLE FROM THE FRONT

This is probably the most common form of tackle used in soccer. An opponent dribbling the ball is coming more or less straight at you, or you are moving straight toward him. Either way, you are going to meet face to face, so your tackle will be delivered to his front.

The first thing you must do is to watch the hips and thighs of the opponent as he comes toward you. If you are looking at this part of him you will keep the ball within your range of sight. More importantly, in the split seconds before you actually go into the tackle, any hip movement he makes will give you early warning that he is going to try to change direction. A smart opponent will always try to tempt you into the tackle, so that he can fool you by some unexpected move.

Once you've made up your mind to tackle, then proceed as follows:

1. Go in with knees slightly bent and body slightly crouched. Keep your arms by your side to avoid being accused of pushing or elbowing your opponent.
2. Get your nontackling foot down right beside the ball.
3. Turn your tackling foot outward so that you can force the whole of the inside edge of your foot against the middle of the ball to block it and then stop its forward progress by leaning into the tackle (fig. 39).

Fig. 39 Block tackle i. The block.

At this point in the tackle, the ball is wedged between your foot and your opponent's foot, and you now have to go through with the tackle to ensure that you get the ball. The advantage is normally with the tackler because he is already powering forward, while his opponent's forward movement has either slowed very considerably, or stopped altogether, as he attempts to keep control of the ball. You, then, must continue to apply maximum force to complete your tackle in one of the following ways:

1. Push the ball through the gap between your opponent's feet (fig. 40).
2. Nudge the opponent's shoulder with your own shoulder so that he falls away from the tackle, leaving you in possession of the ball.
3. Bring the ball sideways out of the tackle. The ball must be pushed over the opponent's foot or rebounded off his foot or shin, so that it comes away sideways, in your possession.

Whichever way it happens, you are on your feet, and you have now got the ball—the two results of a successful tackle.

Summing up those points, you must,

1. watch the opponent's hips and legs as he comes toward you;
2. get your nontackling foot beside the ball and block the ball with the inside of your tackling foot; and
3. go right through with the tackle, i.e., keep forcing your tackling foot forward, using all your body weight to do so, until you come out of the tackle with the ball at your feet.

ALWAYS go into a tackle intending to come out of it with the ball and act as if you are going to do so. Determination is fifty percent of the secret of success in tackling. Tackle with your whole body's weight so that your opponent knows that he's being tackled by something. It has been said of many of the really great tacklers in soccer,

Fig. 40 Block tackle ii. Forcing the ball through between the
opponent's feet.

"When he tackles you, you stay tackled," and "When he tackles you, it's like colliding with a bulldozer," or, "He comes into the tackle like a ton of bricks." These players all played very clean soccer, but they played it hard in the tackle, because that's the way to do it and win.

BLOCK TACKLE FROM THE SIDE

Sometimes an opponent with the ball will be on the move and you will be unable to get in front of him, but must approach from the side. In such cases you use the *block tackle from the side* (fig. 41).

Fig. 41

For this tackle you must approach your opponent from the side, getting the nontackling foot in close to the ball and then pivoting on that foot to bring yourself into a front block tackling position. This probably sounds very complicated if you've never tried it, but if you get someone to stand still with a ball at his feet while you walk in from either side, you will soon see how it works. The diagram shows the tackler approaching from the opponent's right side. He edges his left foot in close to the ball, and pivots on it to bring himself around until he is more or less facing the opponent. He then brings his right foot in to make a front block tackle.

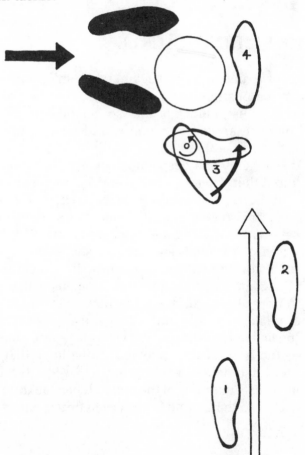

The main points to remember about this tackle are, first, the importance of timing. Seeing you coming, the opponent might put on a burst of speed to take him out of the range of your tackle. So judge the exact moment carefully! Also, get close to your opponent before actually making the tackle. This will help you judge the right moment for your tackle and allow you to get some body weight behind it. If you do not get in close enough, you will be merely stretching out a leg and pushing a foot into the tackle. The tackle will not be firm and will be easily "ridden" by the opponent without disturbing his control of the ball.

THE SLIDING TACKLE

There comes a time, now and again, when an opponent is moving into a position to score, and you just cannot get near enough to use a block tackle. To rob the opponent of the ball on such an occasion you would have to use the sliding tackle (fig. 42).

This is a tackle of a desperate man. You know before you go into it that you are going to end up on the ground, without any hope of controlling the ball. Often, too, you will graze or bruise your skin. This tackle was developed in Europe—mainly in England—where for two-thirds of the soccer season the fields are very wet, soft, and slippery. Under such conditions you can slide into tackles all through the game and the worst that happens is that you get very muddy. On hard, dry fields, however, bare thighs and arms are more readily hurt. What you are trying to do in a sliding tackle is to slide on the knee of the nontackling leg across the front of the opponent in the hope that the foot of the outstretched tackling leg will push the ball away from him. Since most of the outstretched tackling leg is in contact with the ground from start to finish, and since

Fig. 42 Sliding tackle. The tackler has taken the ball right off the
foot of the dribbler. He has not secured the ball for himself
but he has dispossessed his opponent.

the slide must cover two to four yards, it is easy to understand why hard, dry surfaces present special risks.

Once again, timing is crucial. If the tackler goes in too early, he will glide across the front of his opponent, who will then collide with the tackler's upper body. This would sweep the opponent's legs from under him and cause a very heavy fall. If the tackler goes in fractionally late, the sole of the foot, with all his cleats exposed, will go behind the ball and straight into the opponent's legs, making contact somewhere around the ankle, or lower shin—and that is a real leg breaker! Sliding tackles should be left to really experienced players whose timing is good enough to ensure that they do not injure their opponents.

TACKLING FROM THE REAR

If you are chasing after an opponent who has the ball and if there is no one in front or to the side of him to make a tackle, you might try to tackle him from the rear. Tackling from the rear is a matter over which there is much difference of opinion. In the English soccer leagues several rear tackles occur in every match that is played. In some other countries, referees automatically call foul on any attempt to tackle from the rear. They do so because they consider that the mechanics of a rear tackle make it impossible for the tackler to get a foot into a position where it can contact the ball without tripping the opponent. In Britain, a different view is taken: if the tackler's foot plays the ball, any other contact is accidental and therefore not a foul. This may be so. But some very bad fouls occur in British football because tackling from the rear is *not* an automatic foul. Tacklers who have no chance at all of playing the ball come in from the rear and slam their foot, or both feet, into the back of the legs of the opponent. They know full well that there is no chance of playing the ball, but they pretend that they think there is a chance and that they have only

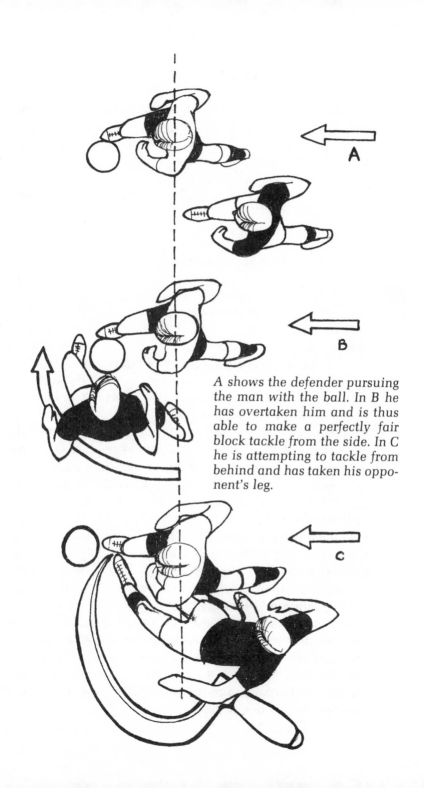

A shows the defender pursuing the man with the ball. In B he has overtaken him and is thus able to make a perfectly fair block tackle from the side. In C he is attempting to tackle from behind and has taken his opponent's leg.

mistimed the tackle. They thus succeed in stopping their opponent, and often in injuring him. It is to be hoped that as soccer develops in the United States this sort of tackle will be very firmly penalized by referees. Tackling from the rear permits the talented player to be stopped by unfair tactics—and there is no point in learning to play well if you can be arbitrarily chopped down by unskilled opponents.

SOME GENERAL ADVICE ON TACKLING

One of the great arts in tackling is knowing *when* to go in and make the tackle. If you could be sure that you would win the ball every time you went into a tackle, you would have nothing to worry about. Opponents, however, as you will have read in the section which deals with "two on one" situations, constantly try to tempt a defender to commit timing errors. When this happens, the attacker, by fooling the defender and taking the ball around him, has taken the defender out of the game. Defenders must learn to prevent this from happening to them.

Attackers will use all sorts of tricks to fool you. They will "show you the ball." This means that when dribbling, an attacker will push the ball a little bit farther from his foot than is normal. Seeing this, you think he's lost control of the ball, when, really, the attacker still has the ball well within reach of his foot. As you come into the tackle he pulls the ball away, leaving you tackling nothing.

Sometimes, players will run at less than top speed while dribbling. You watch, judge, and carefully choose the spot where your foot will meet and capture the ball, and then go into the tackle. As you do so, the attacker will suddenly change pace and move at top speed—or suddenly stop as you come into the tackle. The result is the same—you are left to tackle nothing!

PRACTICE DRILLS FOR TACKLING

Opposed Number Passing

This is exactly the same as Number Passing, which is one of the earliest passing practices, the only difference being that there are two teams with three, four, or five in each. If we call the teams Red and Blue, then Red 1 marks Blue 1, while Red 2 marks Blue 2, and so on. If Reds start with the ball, Red 1 keeps it until Red 2 calls his number. When Red 1 passes to Red 2, Red 3 calls Red 2's number, and so on through the team. However, each of the Reds is marked by his opposite number on the Blue team, so that when Red 2 calls for the ball, Blue 2 knows that he must try to intercept the pass before it gets to Red 2 — or tackle him when he has got it. Each marker is keeping close to his man, trying to stop him from receiving a pass, trying to take the ball from him by tackling when he gets it, and generally making life difficult for him. The attackers, on the other hand, are trying to get away from their markers, and are not calling for the ball until they are certain they can safely receive the pass.

This game, which in the early stages should be limited to three players on each team, is great for developing accurate passing — passes delivered with the right "weight" on them, quick, neat ball control, good running off the ball, and sensible calling for the ball. For the defenders it promotes good marking, shepherding, decisive interception of passes, and firm, well-timed tackling.

Goalkeeping

The problem with training to be a good goalkeeper is that your function is unique. While there are ten other players who must practice using their feet, heads, chests, and knees, but not their hands, you alone as a goalie must practice *handling* the ball in all sorts of different situations.

Basically, the goalie is there to defend the goal—to stop the ball going into the goal—and there are three ways that this is done. The ball may be caught, or otherwise smothered; it may be knocked clear of the goal; or, if the goalie is unable to apply any force, it may be deflected off its course. There are, therefore, two important skills that the young goalie must learn and they are handling and positioning. Of the two, positioning is the more important because good handling is a fairly natural skill to most people, while positioning has to be studied and learned. Unless a goalie is in the right position to reach the ball, the best handling in the world will not save a goal. So, let us think first about positioning.

According to the rules of soccer, a goal is twenty-four feet long and eight feet high. For young players this is usually reduced to twenty-one feet by seven feet. If you look at a goal with a goalkeeper standing in the center of it, the area the goalie is unable to cover is much greater than the area that he *can* cover. This is the view that your opponent, who is about to shoot for goal, has of the situation. Even if you allow for the additional area that the goalie can cover by jumping upward or diving sideways, there is still a large area on either side of him that he cannot possibly get to from his central position on the goal line. Thus, the opponent can choose the spot to aim at, knowing in advance that the goalie is probably not going to be able to stop the ball.

This, figure 44, is how a player who is taking a penalty kick sees the goalie in his goal and this is why nearly

Fig. 44

all penalty kicks (taken from a spot twelve yards in front of the goal) result in a scored goal. The goalie, who is forced by the rules to stand still on the goal line until the ball has been kicked, cannot cover enough of the face of the goal to give himself any chance of stopping a well-directed shot. A penalty kick is a free shot at goal. A good kicker will make every penalty kick into a free goal, and so the first lesson the young goalie must learn is not to give the shooter a similar advantage during the normal course of the game. If the shooter is more or less in front of goal, the goalie must move forward, toward him, for perhaps two yards. This immediately "closes up" the goal to the shooter, because the goalie is now covering more of it (fig. 45). The closer the goalie gets to the shooter, the more of the goal he closes off, until he gets to a point where he has almost closed it off altogether (fig. 46).

This does not mean that the goalie must go rushing forward every time it looks as if someone might shoot at goal. The farther out of the goal the goalie moves, the easier it is for a shooter to lob or chip the ball over the goalie's head and into the goal. When, however, an attack on goal is developing, the goalie should be nearer to the six-yard line than to his goal line. By doing this he is closing a large part of the goal off to all the attackers, and is putting himself in the best position to deal with a shot. If a goal looks well defended and closed up by the goalie, the attacker will probably try to make a pass rather than a shot—which is exactly what you want him to do. If, on the other hand, the goalie is on the goal line, the goal looks big and inviting, and the attacker is liable to take a shot. A good goalkeeper will *save* a shot, but a better goalie will, by good positioning, *prevent the shot from being made!* Remember this: The team that doesn't shoot doesn't score, and the team that doesn't score cannot win.

Exactly the same thing applies when the attacker is somewhere to the side, rather than in front of goal. If you

Fig. 45

Fig. 46

get into the wrong position, you give him a big, inviting goal area to shoot at and score in.

If, however, you move to the side of the goal where the shot is coming from, and then move forward toward the shooter, you can completely block out the goal from his sight. There is not much danger that the ball will be lobbed

over the goalie's head from the side, because the angle is too fine. The danger here lies in having the ball pushed across the front of you, in the form of a pass to another attacker who is running in on goal from the other side. By going to one side of your goal you have left the other side completely open. Every goalie should have an understanding with his backs so that whenever the goalie goes across his goal to cover one side, a back will cover the other side of the goal.

When you need to cover the possibility of a shot from the side, move to the near goalpost and then move forward (out of goal), until you cannot quite touch the post with your outstretched hand (fig. 47), and your position will be approximately correct. You would then make minor adjustments in your position depending on where the man with the ball is.

Fig. 47

What you have is a sort of flat arc across the front of the goal, around which the goalie will move when his goal is threatened. He will be constantly placing himself between the ball and his goal, blocking off as much of his goal as possible from the attacker.

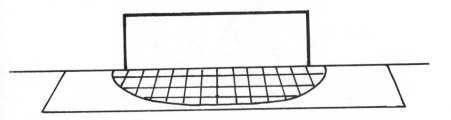

This will put the goalie in the best position to deal with any shots which are fired at his goal. Now and again, however, an attacker will break through the defense and come racing in on the goal with the ball at his feet, and there will be no one to stop him except the goalie. In this situation the goalie knows that there are only two things the attacker can do. He can either try to *shoot* the ball past the goalie into the goal, or he can try to dribble it round the goalie and *push* it into the goal. Whichever the attacker wants to do, the goalie must, at least, make it difficult for him—and in the end try to stop him from doing either. The goalie must come out of his goal and go straight at the attacker, and he must do it quickly. If the goalie comes out first, he forces the attacker to act quickly, and this alone will often force a mistake. As the goalie goes forward toward the attacker, every step he takes blocks off the goal a bit more. Eventually he might close off the goal so completely that the attacker no longer has the choice of shooting or dribbling—he has got to dribble and the goalie knows this. When you know what your opponent is going to do, the situation becomes that much easier to deal with.

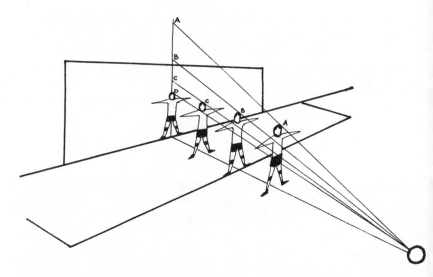

As the goalkeeper moves forward he eventually gets to a point where any ball going over his head will also go over the cross bar. (See Lines A and B) The same applies to either side of him. He gets to a point that any ball passing to the side of him will miss the goal. (See 1 and 2) It should be remembered however that the further out of his goal the goalkeeper comes the more vulnerable he is to the ball which is chipped or lobbed over his head.

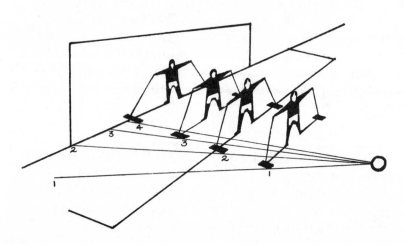

Once you know he is going to try to dribble the ball around you, just throw yourself down on the ball and clutch it to you. This might sound dangerous, but if you go in hard, without hesitating, and try to get your back into the attacker's legs as you go down, you will not come to much harm. Watch the ball as you go in and down to secure it. Pull it into your body as soon as you have got your hands on it (fig. 48).

Fig. 48

The actual handling skills come more naturally than the kicking skills. Most shots will come in at you in one of four ways.

1. Low—along the ground
2. Higher—up to shoulder height
3. Higher still—so that you have to jump to get the ball
4. Out of reach to the side—requiring a diving grasp at the ball

THE LOW SHOT

A ball coming at you along the ground, or close to it, should always be gathered from a kneeling position. In this position (fig. 49) the hands are the first line of defense, but if, by chance, the ball beats the hands, the legs form a

Fig. 49

second line of defense to stop its going past you and into the goal. The goalkeeper drops onto one knee and watches the ball come right into his hands. He allows the ball to come to his hands rather than reaching out and grabbing it, and as soon as he has his hands around the ball he pulls it into his stomach. His whole body forms a curve into which the ball is cradled.

THE HIGHER SHOT

It is always important in goalkeeping to get some part of your body right behind your hands, to act as a second line of defense. When the ball is coming at you at waist, chest, or shoulder height, it is reasonably easy to get your trunk behind your hands and pull the ball into the cradle of the chest and stomach. If the ball is slightly below waist height, the goalie will have to bend his knees enough to allow the ball to come into hands which are held in front of the stomach. If the ball is at chest or shoulder height, the goalie will have to get up onto his toes or even jump in order to clutch the ball in against his stomach. As with the low shot, you should allow the ball to come to your hands, not reach out to catch it with extended arms. Let the ball come into the cradle formed by the chest and stomach and then wrap the hands around it (fig. 50). With the ball firmly cradled in your arms and protected by your body, it is not likely to jump out if an attacker jostles you as you catch it.

DEALING WITH THE HIGH BALL

This is necessary when the ball comes in high—at well over head height. This means that you've got to jump to catch it. It can happen in two ways—first, when a rising shot is coming in and, second, when a high ball is coming across or onto the goal and the goalie must get it before

Fig. 50

someone else does! Whichever way it happens, the technique is the same. Watch the ball, time your jump, and stretch the arms up as far as possible so that you get your hands to the side and back of the ball. The thumbs should be almost touching at the back of the ball. The ball should be caught while it is still in front of the head, and thus well within the field of vision (fig. 51). In other words, the goalie should never lose sight of the ball; he should be able to watch it right into his hands. As soon as he has the ball in his hands he should pull it down to his stomach and cradle it. It is important to pull the ball down quickly because while the arms are extended there is no second line of defense behind the hands. Without this, accidental contact with another player—either while the goalie is up in the air, or as he lands—could cause the goalie to lose the ball.

Sometimes it is wiser not to attempt to catch the high ball, but to either deflect it over the crossbar or to knock it away, usually by punching it. This will occur when the goalie has to jump for a ball with a group of other players, some of whom are attackers. In this situation, although he might get his hands around the ball, he would not be certain of being able to hold it. Also, he doesn't know how he will land—another possible threat to ball control. If the ball is coming in on goal at a considerable speed, he can, by putting one or both hands under the ball, push it upward so that it passes safely over the crossbar. He has given away a corner kick to his opponents, but he has made his goal safe.

If, however, the approaching shot is a dropping ball or one which is coming across the goal rather than in on goal, then it is very difficult to push the ball over the crossbar. In such cases, the goalie would be better advised to punch the ball away from the immediate danger area in front of his goal. Goalkeepers should try, when punching, to make the contact with the knuckles of both fists together, and to punch right through the center of the ball (fig. 52). If it is impossible to get both hands to the ball, then contact

Fig. 51

Fig. 52

should be made with the knuckles of one hand. Some goalies are able to punch a ball twenty yards or more this way, and that, for a punched ball, is a good clearance. The kind of contact the goalie is able to make with the ball depends largely on how many players are going up together for it, and how well or badly the goalie was placed when he went into his jump. If the goalie is able to jump right underneath the ball, he can choose what he wants to do, because he has the length of his arms as an advantage over all the other players, who are not allowed to touch the ball with their hands (fig. 53). If, however, there are two other players between him and the ball, the goalkeeper will be pleased if he is able to get a good one-handed punch at it. In such circumstances, the goalie will often have to punch with the side of his fist and be content with knocking the ball away sideways, merely to get it away from the immediate danger area in front of his goal. This is a fairly desperate measure because the goalie can neither clear the ball away far enough to give his team time to reorganize their defense before another attack comes in, nor can he be certain where or to whom the ball will go—it might go straight to another attacker who will shoot it back at goal almost before the goalie has got his feet back on the ground! Whatever happens however, it is better than missing it altogether in the most dangerous area of the field— right in front of your own goal!

DIVING FOR THE BALL

It is an old soccer saying that "A good goalie doesn't have to throw himself about; he gets into the right position before the shot is made and can catch the ball with both his feet on the ground." Like a lot of old sayings, there is some truth in this: many of the diving saves seen in soccer matches would not have been necessary if the goalie had been where he should have been when the shot was made.

Fig. 53

But, again, like a lot of old sayings, it is only true up to a point. You can be an expert positioning goalie and still have to make diving saves. What else can you do when you are unsighted and don't see the shot being made—your first sight of the ball might occur when it is on its way toward the corner of your goal! Or when you have positioned yourself perfectly to take a shot, which is then deflected off another player and changes course on its way to goal! The only way to deal with situations like these is to dive for the ball. Of course, goalies are human, too, and a misjudgment or a mistake might also necessitate diving for the ball.

When making a diving save, try to catch the ball while you are in midair; otherwise you have to be satisfied with getting one hand to the ball and keeping it out of the goal by pushing it away. In another kind of diving save the goalie throws himself sideways in order to get down and smother the ball. This is normally more of a falling than a diving action. The goalie knows that he can get to the ball, so, watching it all the time, he pushes himself into a sideways fall, and as he reaches the ground he stretches out and grasps the ball with both hands, pulling it in to his chest and stomach (fig. 54). This is the type of diving save that a goalie would normally choose to make rather than trying to jump sideways and then drop onto one knee to gather the ball—which would take much longer to do. The two important points are, first, to go down on your side rather than on the chest and stomach, and, then, to get your hands behind the ball and pull it into your body quickly. In the true diving save the goalie throws himself sideways through the air to try to catch a ball or to push it sideways to keep it out of the goal (fig. 55). When you have to do this, if you are able you should get your hands around the ball while you are still in the air, and pull it into your chest quickly, so that you have got it firmly against the front of your body when you hit the ground. The impact, as you land, could easily cause the ball to jump out of your hands

Fig. 54

Fig. 55

if they are still outstretched. Try to land on your side because landings on the chest and stomach are painful and likely to knock all the breath out of you—especially if you've pulled the ball in, and then land on it. If you are unable to catch the ball but are able to get a hand to it and push it away, you should—even as you are falling to the ground—watch where it has gone. If it is still in play, bounce up onto your feet as soon as you hit the ground, and be ready, because it will probably be on its way back to goal by then.

In addition to handling practice, goalkeepers should also practice ball distribution. When a goalie gets the ball in his hands, he has ten players on his own team in front of him, and he has to get the ball safely to one of them. He might need to give a short, quick pass to a defender, or he might need to send the ball half the length of the field to an attacker, but whatever he does, it must be done accurately and, when necessary, quickly. The goalie must be able to throw a ball to a teammate, to roll it, or to kick it. Some goalies can throw a ball almost as far as they can kick it, and this is a very useful skill to have, because a throw can be delivered much faster than the types of kick that goal-keepers tend to use, and with much more accuracy over a long distance.

The two types of kick mainly used by goalies are the punt and the placekick. The placekicking technique is described in the "Kicking" chapter.

THE PUNT

This is, historically, the oldest form of kicking in football games of all kinds; it is the only form of kicking which is still used in all forms of football—American, Rugby, Soc-cer, Australian Rules, Gaelic, and so on. If you've played any football and you can punt a football, you can punt a soccer ball, because the technique is exactly the same.

The ball is held in both hands with the arms extended downward. The head is down watching the ball. As the kicking leg starts to swing forward, the ball is released, and the kicking leg straightens with a fast, powerful action as contact is made with the ball (fig. 56). The head is kept down after the ball has been kicked and a full follow-through of the kicking leg is permitted. Almost anyone can punt a ball a long distance, given a little practice, but it takes a lot of practice to kick the ball over the required distances with the necessary accuracy to ensure that the ball always goes to a teammate, and never to an opponent.

Fig. 56

THE GOAL KICK

It is very important for every goalkeeper to be able to kick a "dead" ball well, because during the course of a game he will have to take several goal kicks: the ball is placed on a spot within the goal area, and from there it is kicked into play. The goalie normally takes these kicks, so it is necessary for him to be able to hit a good long ball from the spot—to the halfway line, or farther—with a fair degree of accuracy. A goal kick should be a long pass to a teammate. We have already dealt with this type of kick in the section that deals with kicking, but, briefly, the nonkicking foot is slightly behind the ball, and the ball is hit with the laces of the boot (the instep) at a point slightly below the midline of the ball, so that the ball will rise. Use a full follow-through with the kicking leg after contact with the ball.

PRACTICE DRILLS
FOR GOALKEEPING

As we have said before, the practice drills which are good for the rest of the team are not really suitable for the goalie. By far the best practice is obtained by having three or four players stand around the edge of the penalty area (or about eighteen–twenty yards from your goal), firing shots at you, one at a time.

At first, it is better for both you and the shooters to pay more attention to where the ball is kicked than to how hard. Tell them what sort of ball you want, for instance, "Keep it low and to my right," or, "Put them all in to my left." This will allow you to concentrate on gathering low balls, or to get some jumping and diving practice. You can also ask teammates to throw high balls into goal to allow you to practice catching and turning them over the crossbar. It is, however, almost impossible for your teammates to kick accurately enough to put every ball exactly where you need it to receive the right practice.

Another very useful drill for sharpening your movements and making you more agile requires two or three teammates standing level with the penalty spot. Let them throw (underarm) balls into the goal at various heights and to the left or right of you. As you save each ball, or as it goes over the goal line, the next one is thrown, so that you, in the goal, are on the move all the time, dealing with ball after ball in quick succession.

Do join in the kicking practices with the rest of the team—you need to be a good kicker. Practice placekicking and punting for distance and accuracy. Give yourself a target to aim at—another player (who can kick the ball back to you), or a circle marked on the ground—and try to hit it ten times out of ten.

Another good game to play requires that two of you stand at an equal distance from a center line. One kicks the ball and the other catches it. Having caught it, the second man can then kick it from the place where he caught it. If he fails to catch it, he must kick it from five yards behind the place where the ball hit the ground. What each player is trying to do is to drive the other back until he goes across the end line. A soccer field is ideal for this game.

Glossary of Common Soccer Terms

Back: a player whose role is mainly defensive

Bend (the ball): to kick the ball so that it swerves in flight

Center (the ball): to make a pass from a wide position to the center of the field, near to goal (This is also called "crossing" the ball.)

Clearance: usually a kick, but sometimes a header which sends the ball clear of your own goal area

Corner Kick: When a player plays the ball and it goes out of play over his own goal line, but outside the goal, the other team restarts the game by taking a free kick from the small arc at the corner flag, on whichever side of the goal the ball went over the goal line.

Dead ball: the ball when stationary—as it would be preceding a free kick

Far post: The goalpost farther away from the player with the ball

FIFA: initials of Fédération Internationale de Football Association, the world governing body of soccer

First time: playing the ball as it comes to you without first attempting to control it (This usually refers to passing or shooting at goal.)

Follow-through: when kicking the ball, allowing the kicking leg to continue with the kicking action after contact with the ball has ceased

Forward: a front-line attacking player—a striker or a winger.

Free kick: a dead-ball kick awarded to a team on account of an infringement of the rules by their opponents, who are not permitted to be closer than ten yards from the ball when the kick is taken. A free kick can be direct, which means that a goal may be scored with the kick, or indirect, when a goal may not be scored directly from the kick.

Goal area: sometimes called "the six-yard box" (see plan of pitch)

Goal kick: a dead-ball kick taken from within the goal area to restart play after the attacking team has played the ball over the goal line without scoring a goal (The kick is normally taken by the goalkeeper.)

Goalside: between an attacker and the goal you are defending, or, if you are the attacker, between the defender and his goal

Half: a team's half of the field is the half which contains the goal which that team is defending. The other half of the field is their opponents' half.

Inswinger: a center, or a corner kick executed in a way which bends it inward, toward the goal

Kickoff: a kick from the center spot that either starts a game, or restarts it after a goal or halftime

Lob: a short, high kick, usually made to send the ball over the head of an opponent

Mark (an opponent): to stay close to an opponent when you

are in defense, to try to ensure that he does not get the ball, or if he does, that he is prevented from doing anything useful with it

Midfield (player, sometimes called "Link"): a player whose function can be both defensive and offensive, but is primarily to set up attacks for his own forwards and to prevent the other team's midfield from doing the same for their forwards (The team that controls the middle of the field should win the match.)

NASL: initials of the North American Soccer League, the nationwide professional league

Near post: the goalpost nearer to the player with the ball

Offside: a technical type of foul which occurs when a player who is in his opponents' half of the field has less than two opponents between him and the goal he is attacking when a teammate plays the ball

Outswinger (see Inswinger): in this case, the ball bends outward, away from the goal

Penalty area: the eighteen-yard by forty-four-yard area in front of the goal (Any foul on the person which is committed inside this box is punished by the award of a penalty kick, which may be taken by any member of the offended team.)

Penalty kick: a direct free kick awarded as a result of a foul on the person of an attacker inside the penalty area (The kick is taken from the penalty spot.)

Penalty spot: a spot marked twelve yards in front of the goal, from which penalty kicks are taken

Return pass: a pass which is made directly back to the player who originally passed it (This type of pass is used in the wall pass situation.)

Running off the ball: running without the ball to get into a position to receive a pass, or to support a teammate, or to distract your opponents by running as a decoy

Shepherd: to make an attacker go in a specific direction (This is sometimes called "jockeying.")

Shielding or Screening (the ball): keeping one's body between a defender and the ball to prevent him from
making a tackle or other attempt to take the ball away

Square ball: a pass which goes across the field

Stand off: in defense, to refuse to be tempted into a tackle,
but rather to keep goalside of the attacker, backing
away in front of him, keeping him contained (This is
sometimes known as "containing" an attacker.)

Striker: a forward whose main role is to score goals or to act
as a target man

Support (a teammate): running close by a teammate who
has the ball so that he may pass to you if he wishes (In
defense, you support by being near a teammate as he
goes into the tackle, in case he is unsuccessful, in
which case you will have his man covered.)

Sweeper: a specialist back who operates behind the main
line of defense to gather up balls that come through
the main line (He "sweeps up" behind the other
backs.)

Target man: a striker, normally a big man, at whom long
passes, mostly through the air, are directed (The target
man is expected to pass the ball off very quickly to a
teammate, probably using a header. A mobile target
man can make life very difficult for any defense, and
other players will score many goals from his passes.)

Through ball: a pass that is hit more or less straight forward, in an attempt to get a ball through the main line
of backs, with a striker chasing it

Throw-in: the method of bringing the ball back into play
when it has passed over the touchline (A player from
the team which did not play the ball over the
touchline throws the ball back into the playing area,
using a two-handed throw, releasing the ball when it
is over his head—figure 57.)

Touchline: see field diagram (p.4)

Unsighted: when a player, particularly a goalie, cannot see

the ball as it is played, or loses sight of it as it travels

Wall: a line of players, positioned ten yards in front of the ball at a free kick to block the goal

Weight (of a pass): the amount of force with which the ball arrives. (The greater the weight on the ball, the more difficult it is to control. Getting the right weight on a pass is almost as important as its accuracy.)

Winger: an attacking player who usually operates near the touchline.

Fig. 57